Buckshot Reckoning

Poems by Mike Jurkovic

LUCHADOR
PRESS

Luchdor Press
Big Tuna, TX

Copyright © Mike Jurkovic, 2023

First Edition: 1 3 5 7 9 10 8 6 4 2

ISBN: 978-1-958182-44-4

LCCN: 20239300

Cover art: Emily Monahan

Forensic doodling: Mike Jurkovic

Back Cover photo: *Poet In a Box* (Alcatraz, 2004)- Emily Monahan

Author photo: Mike Jurkovic

"Not least because of his heroic efforts on behalf of the art through his leadership of Calling All Poets, Mike Jurkovic is rightly something of a local legend—especially in the sense that we all need a legend to interpret the map. From the profoundly moving first poem, "Blood Street," to the fasci-nating account of "My Meeting w/ Vonnegut" and beyond, *Buckshot Reckoning* richly delivers on its promise of what he calls mishap and magic. In his latest affable, shrewd, and politically acute collection, we find a kindred spirit to the Kerouac of *Mexico City Blues*, poems overflowing with what Kerouac described as Love's multitudinous boneyard of decay / The spilled milk of heroes."

- Thomas Festa, Professor of English, SUNY New Paltz, author of *Earthen*

"Bravely and boldly, Jurkovic announces the second scene/ of the third act. In *Buckshot Reckoning* the poet confronts both mortality and criminality as he confesses that the age/of repair/ is upon me. Such repair is difficult in the context of a world gone batshit but that difficulty is exactly what Jurkovic engages with. The poems are clearly influenced by the poet's deep involvement with music either as directly alluded to (Screaming Jay Hawkins and Me in Our Prime) or in poems like crack n stack in which the repetition and cadence suggest a musical performance, as if the poet and the poem are about to leap off the stage and start a performance right in front of us. There is huge range in these poems – memories of youth and sex and excitement bump up against the terrors of the present moment – the drift and wreckage/ wreckage and grift of a world gone mad with poison and war. And then there is the quieter despair that comes with facing illness and loss, a life in which the speaker describes perfecting daily/the coffin pose. This is a brave book, that pulls no punches. Life and aging are just plain hard."

- Ruth Danon, Creative & Expository Writing Coordinator, CMcGhee Division, New York University; Author of *Turn Up the Heat*

"Mike Jurkovic's keen eye, sharp ear and compassionate heart beckon us once again--and reward us with uniquely satisfying images: from crimps in the human foil to tannins of peace. Gift yourself with this thoughtful and provocative book.

   - Irene O'Garden, poet, author, *Risking the Rapids,*
    Off-Broadway playwright, *Women On Fire*

"Buckshot Reckoning, while embracing his distinctive dark humor, marries wicked with, often dis-guised, tenderness to create a collection that confronts, questions & surprises – the kind of poetry we wish for but rarely find in print."

   - Roger Aplon, editor & publisher *Waymark - a poetry*
    Magazine. Author: *Mustering What's Left - Selected & New*
    Poems 1976-2017, and *The Omnipotent Sorcerer*

"He's the mad house jester whose jabs jolt and sting. As one poem puts it, gravity gets us all which is as serious as it gets. Enjoy this work, it is original and a pleasure to read."

   - Guy Reed, poet, *The Effort to Hold Light, Second Innocence*

Acknowledgments:

"Clock of Things" - *Monnstone Arts Center Featured Readers 2022 Anthology,* "Color Code" - *Lightwood: life and the arts in the 21st century* - Winter, 2023, "Downtown Comedy Legends" - *Gasconade Review,* 2023, "droopy old pine" (first published as "Two Months Before Leaving") - *Chronogram 2003, The Country and Abroad, 2005,*"Eastern Painted" - *Lightwood: life and the arts in the 21st century* - Winter, 2023, "(h)ours" - *Lightwood: life and the arts in the 21st century* -Winter, 2023, "in a room above a deli on the corner in a dream" - *Brownstone Poets Anthology* 2021, "My Sister" – *Linden Avenue Literary Review,* 2016, "Old Man Maneri's Typing Class" - *Poetry Super Highway,* April, 2021 (older version), "Screaming Jay Hawkins and Me in Our Prime" – *Panolopyzine,* 2016. (Pushcart Nominee), "tinker less (2.0)" - originally published as "tinkerless" - *Packingtown Review*, Fall, 2020, "That Picture of Her In Her Prime (dashing cameraman)" - *Chronogram,* December, 2022, "The Girl and Her Parachute" – *Main Street Rag,* 2014, *Gasconade Review,* 2023 , "Yearbook" - *Gasconade Review,* 2023

TABLE OF CONTENTS

I'd change her sad rags into glad rags if I could

-"Rag Doll" (Bob Crewe & Bob Gaudio)

for Emily, forever

Blood Street

It was raining on the Red Lights on Bloedstraat
when I heard they found your remains
thirty five hundred miles away
in the woods in Massachusetts.

We had only met maybe twice
once during a radio interview for my book
which was new at the time
but not since. You liked my haiku
and I thanked you for that.

Now they've found your remains
thirty five hundred miles from back there
and it doesn't seem right. Perhaps,
like so much, there should have been
more: refuge, shelter. And maybe the rain
on the Red Lights will wash it all away but
I doubt things like forgiveness and mercy
in times like these.

In a room above a deli on the corner
in a dream

Christmas lights kindle
the morning civics at Molly's
as Jack swears *Jimmy was
the best barkeep ever*
and you nod yeah cos
you're new in town
and don't yet know
the whole borough truth
but you swear
on your mother's grave
you know these guys
from the room
above a deli
on the corner
in a dream
from a room
above a deli
on the corner
in a dream
And you really need
some down time
but the devil
(and his deep state)
have other plans
for you boyo
In a room

above a deli

on the corner

in a dream

In a room

above a deli

on the corner

in a dream

Downtown Comedy Legends

Rummy Blinks and Gravel Duck would never be
the downtown comedy legends they sought to be
cos they stayed plush dealing dust and favors
for Toady Morocco, a South Side pimp
who ran his ten blocks w/a gunner's gaze,

I wouldn't fuck your sister for those two
he said w/o haste and a benzedrine bray.
But they do what you ask
ya can't fuck em for that.

Rummy Blinks and Gravel Duck
were a seedy thesis
to pare this poem around
but, like the heated city,
a thesis just the same:
of drift and wreckage.
Wreckage and grift.

Clock of Things

No lichen on my pizza please
but she insists like new york girls do
when they know they're right
and you're just a doofus staring, staring
at . . .Well they know you know they know
what you're staring at and they're gonna
have their way no matter the day
of the week
or the month
of the minute
in the larger
clock of things
that chimes
the hours of
the avalanche
that overwhelms
even we
who once
outpaced
the curve.

Eleanor's Purse

Eleanor's purse held many things.
Everyone's prone to the shivers and yips
she says, curating her bag
w/a passion few possess.
This here's for bloating she'd puff,
holding a change of face and coin
one small vial, two orange pills,
three sets of sixty, four counts of felony,
five minor headaches, six Christmas trees,
seven separate somethings.
Eight triple ply, nine bold remarks,
ten turtle doves, eleven assorted mints
twelve novellas, and

You lose at least ninety minutes of life
stuck in traffic each day she'd insist,
no stranger to the truth but not quite kin.

God wields w/o partiality
she'd note, handing you a hammer.

crack n stack

In dream seventy-nine my idiot son balances
empty Super 8 movie reels in a box on his head
while snapping plastic hangers in two
and stacking them into neat little piles.
Crack n stack. Crack n stack. 24/7.
It was maddening, truly, and I had no way to stop him.
All day long on into the night I'd yell, I'd plead,
I'd seek professional council but to no avail.
Crack n stack. Crack n stack. Home,
away, relentless. Neat little piles about 6,
maybe 8 inches high. Then he'd knock em all down
and start again. Crack n stack. Crack n stack. 24/7.
I don't even know how the world hung its clothes.

Yearbook

Frost's granddaughter
convinced me of my brilliance
as she held me between her legs
like I was the last poet on earth.

We were young so sex closed the deal.
Rock that girl and you were the next big thing
in the land of lettres. Bite her neck
and she read your words w/worship.

Hell, I could do that.
It was junior year n I
had spunk aplenty.
My tongue 'tween
her cleavage,
her lips on
my belly,
our fingers
tracing sweat.

I had *a way w/alliteration*
that was totally American
she said. My hands on her
feverish ass, foraging for
her fulcrum. Breathing warm along
her panty line. Their color that
of open sky.

The Picture of Her In Her Prime
(the dashing cameraman)

She has taps on her shoes and a tube for later
but that shouldn't deter you from getting to know
her dress, her sex, her titular seam.

She won't give you a yes or no about the tube
but she was never keen on annotation.
Besides that's her kick for later.

But she did get the taps from an Italian down the street
a few years back when such things were in fashion and
she flirted w/the dashing cameraman
who took this picture of her in her prime.

(h)ours

My basement is my Warerloo, my Rubicon,
my Matterhorn. The shore upon which I'll sort
my bins and boxes. Scatter and rant.

Mom's stuff, Dad's stuff. Hearsay, (h)ours.
The everyday hum of meter and sump.
The furies. The seasons. Electric and dark.

By the furnace a forest of oddities: first drafts
and false noses. All debris accounted for.
My last Shangri-La.

Cadence

The stoop was our stage
so step aside and
let this shaman
show you the shuffle
that stops 'em dead
along Fordham Road.
That keeps 'em
comin' back
to East 1 3 8
and the cadence
of the curb
and the cool
of the Corner Boys
crooning in front
of Fatima's Falafel,
her saffron and dill
making sweet
the otherwise
diesel air.

Eastern Painted

The poet's turtle, an Eastern Painted,
paddles like prose. The bard tidies his bonsai,
pulls a thread from a blue cable knit
and leans in. *Sometimes it's more than a floater*
he whittles as Slowboy,
(as awash in fish flakes as the poet in wine)
withdraws his head and considers that he
and the guy biding time via pen
both bear the grimace of studied intent.

She packs umbrellas in her shoes when she flies
he scribes. But it's tentative, not the place
to hang his hat, set down his wine.

This one's a slog thinks Slowboy
through a rabble of bubbles.
Snapping at a passing meal
like the guy in the sweater
bites on verbs. The poet doodles.
His double paddles northward
to see the sky through unkept glass.
In a bit of a brood, the poet too,
drawn to the same wild wonder.

Blue Candle

Here in the heart
of Mea Culpa County,
the girl who helped thunder
had nothing really
to do w/the rain.

She was just a girl
(pronoun/verb)
standing, in the shadow of the cross,
and lit a blue candle
amid the high mountains.

Who knew love's rhombus
proved proverb and vowel.
A girl of infinite clouds,
who had nothing at all
to do with the rain.

flurries expected

There's a quiet
on Third Avenue
this morning
(flurries expected
no more than an inch)
Winter is still
six blocks away
but you can feel it
in your bones:
That bohemian gray
pigeon magic
of Christmas
on 68th.

The Girl and Her Parachute

The girl and her parachute
were a cute enigma
from the moment
she got in my car
six miles awry
of her landing.

Thanks for the ride she said,
her parachute strangely mute.
So unlike my mother-in-law
going rogue in Vegas.

But this isn't about
any mother-in-law
past or present.
This is about the girl
and her parachute,
who could have landed on my car
if the westerlies were true.

*You go for the buzz because
all the rest is bullshit* she said.
And in the sky above Awosting
two clouds were eloping.

Broken Old House

Just down the road
not far from here
a fentanyl coven
of pale crepe vampires
breed in the broken old house
they split into four apartments.
Rat holes certainly
but it's like that here.

Laced w/warheads,
their eyes: In free fall.
Their hair: Black ash.
They torment two rooms
n half a bath. Greet the christened
off the bus. Await the gunshots
sure to come.

Look No Less Upon these Eyes

Cold stone quarries.
The galleries of Golgotha
where curio hounds
exalt the moment.
Rummage their catalog sins.

I am no longer confident enough
to ask directions to the men's room.
I just go where I am
and hope for a mop.
The color of genius:
the pallor of paste.
Oatmeal Venus
the moon is full.

Look no less upon these eyes
as one would road-kill:
the flattened meat
of discursive lust.
The twisted thrust
of fur and bone.
My initials carved into
the tree.

Common Square *(Lexington, 11/2/22)*

The blue wisdom sky
beckons the pilot of dreams,
minute-men and brethren,
to assemble on
this common square
to defend, from w/in this time,
the frightened, the bargained,
the convinced otherwise
that our time, as free men
is gone. That the perfect union
belongs to only one skin,
one god, one torn ragged banner.
To defend, from w/in this time,
those who deem themselves
the only heirs to this land. To defend,
from w/in this time, those who have
deserted this common square and
choose, no long, no pray, no lust
for monarchy, kingship, slavery.
To defend, from w/in this time,
the murderous, and traitorous,
among us.

Guernica

She came from a time
of montage and melee.
Mishap and magic.
A time when women
were favored, not imprisoned
by men who conflate freedom
w/virtue and vengeance.

She came from a time
when the music of the night
was a one hit wonder.
Not the angry drone
of these lesser days
where the ugly no one expected
holds the Magi captive.

She came from a time
before this joyless period
of howl
and wolf
and haunting.
The staggering ring
of soldiers marching.
The scream of mother's
broken sword.

My Sister

In the umbra of banks
beneath humid stars
she serves a tumorous magic.
Labors in sour purpose.
Gives birth to good soldiers
like good girls do.

Screaming Jay Hawkins and Me
in Our Prime

I'm lost in a parking lot on the left coast
w/an Afghan Kush and Grey Goose buzz
when Screamin' Jay Hawkins
jumps the Sierra's screaming:
What can I do w/ eighty-six kids
'n each momma wantin' my jam?!
Get in motherfucker! I salvo,
kicking the gas like a mule bucks gravity.

Hurling down coastal route one
w/an oft-subpoenaed legend in my car
doesn't faze me. Hell no! I expect these things
from time to time: the brain unhinged,
the whole world gone batshit.

Screamin' Jay riffing in the passenger seat
is no more nuts to me than
dumping poisons in the ocean to my left.
Its vast sky full w/the moans of our daughters'
womb engines, pumping out pilots, privates, and warlords
no one believes can win anymore.

What Grove Will Glisten

If, as predicted,
this winter is
the harshest in years,
what chaos of choice
awaits this old forest and me
as it passes into spring?
What trees will fall?
What beliefs will stagger?
What grove will glisten
renewed, intact?

Maggie's Piano

Air colored

blocks

of time

melt the cyanide

in my glass.

Civil War chic

is hot again.

No one respects

the hometown prophet

not even

the girls

who dated him.

Cocktail murmurs

scour the bones.

The roar of colonels

demands men die.

Maggie's piano

holds no song.

droopy old pine

Never gave you
much thought
till now.

You're still the old pine
we never lit w/lights or
picnicked near.

Beneath your height
above peak and soffit
every genus

falls in your shade,
the moon and stars
go about their business.

Your tangle snaps
at my touch, the fire
incandescent.

November(ish)

My work is to clear the path
not set your steps
to the long foreground
no one escapes.
No one improves.

The siege of days
no one does not
give in to: The loss of light
and isolation. The damning chill
of lesser days.

Line of us

Like everything else
　(these loathsome days)
I'm starting from scratch
　(and God knows where)
His wind
　(doth blow)
the whole belligerent line of us
　(who run roughshod)
down the middle
　(until the pills)
go down
　(easier)
each day.
　(The arthritis)
kicks in
　(and the stents)
are placed
　(in what)
passes for pause
　(if not peace)
in this place.

Old Man Maneri's Typing Class

I learned a lot about rhythm
in old man Maneri's typing class.
They're only after your money! he'd bark.
Now's the time for acceptance!
Now is the time for all good men
to come to the aid of their country!

His mealy eyes
punch-holed
like a fossil
and,
click clack
went the class
again
click clack
went the clock
again

The sieged get served cold soup!
he'd cry and,
click clack
went the clock
again
click clack
went the clock
again

60some

Really. Who's to blame me if,
after sixty some years of
 raking leaves, burning leaves
  dragging leaves, bagging leaves
   mulching leaves, blowing leaves
I leave them where they fall this year
and promise to reciprocate
 when the unknown hour arrives
  and my graceless fall
   litters the yard

She makes palm trees faint

She makes palm trees faint.
Plays hopscotch in the mesa.
Takes off her clothes
w/the moon's encouragement
and my eternal gratitude.
Undulates towards the river
like a dolphin swims in awe.

w/Will Nixon

On a grid of mad purpose

Neath the azure sky
above Colorado,
the critic in my head
tells me to sit this one out.
That the contention I carry
(like a grim code
  on a grid of mad purpose)
is bald conjecture at best.

Trigger happy and mobile,
you kiss a lot of ass
on days w/o poets.
Where children gather
under nuclear skies.
Rule or ruin
not withstanding.

handful of whispers

buoyed by your fears
I double the oxy.
A handful of whispers
washes them down.

Color Code *(tanka)*

I've outsourced my brain
to square colored paper blue
tomorrows pink and
soft purple lilac missions
holding fast upon the fridge

Finish Line *(ghostlike, mostly)*

It's the second scene

of the third act

when all hell

breaks loose

and all

the lights

are green

on 3rd Avenue

'n no where else

is the clamor

more effusive,

the harmony

more rent,

than here

at the

finish line

where myths

and gods

convene

to bicker

pipe dream

w/leftover pangs
of contentment,
we craft these fictions
barely scratching
the surface
of our odd
tectonics.

The least becomes
possible,
and all
the rest
a
pipe dream.

Scrivener's Error

is never too far

from the crime scene.

Is written into the contracts

that bind us: the procedures

and prognosis.

The fevers

and firewalls

that siege

our stateless days.

Our correspondence

never too far

from coercion.

The whitewash

of fiction

and form.

Her Finery

Like soot upon her finery
the ash of my nature
alights.

Under surveillance
our talk defers. Science,
sadism. Grey, indifferent,
back burner stuff.

We both know, my antagonist and I,
where the bones are buried.
So we indulge in lesser discourse,
a lesser degree of want.

tinker less *(2.0)*

I'm so prone to forgery
you might think
I wrote this poem
but I didn't.

It rolled in
on a fog
of sleeplessness
from a room
w/a spurious
past.

Beset, I dressed
and came to you,
my blueprint
in need
of revision.

Piece by Piece by Piece

Perhaps we're meant
to leave this place
piece by piece by piece.
Lymph node. Tissue.
Parts diminished. Flaws
exposed. Piece by piece by piece
perfecting daily
the coffin pose
the home crowd sees,
all gussied up
and gone elsewhere
by the time
the wake
concludes.

And Your Crashing Epigrams
(better people's houses)

All your in-laws
hold over you
is your management
of metaphors, minotaurs,
and what you charge
for mini-tours
of better people's
houses. That,
and your crashing
epigrams,
witless and
obtuse.

Battered thin

Here at the tumor summit
everything's so laissez faire,
so in your face
and fathomless
that you
double the espresso,
harness the wifi
and redress all crimps
in the human foil,
battered thin
and shiny.

heaven's flowers

The l e n g t h e n i n g silence
of festive days   stirs not
   heaven's flowers   Quiet
  amongst themselves   they
   bar no access   claim
  no junction   Spray
yon fields   w/mossy wood
  musky blooming apple tree
 Tannins   of   peace,
   relief   and   vale
   The eucalyptus day

consensus omnium

and madness, after all, is a haven of sorts not far from heaven

Raphael Kosek

Poets ache in the strangest places
but we all agree
that scripting madly
  in huts of our own
  illustration

is the only way to savor
the fret and sprawl
of our furious movements

away from absolution.

The Bench

Both now and in motion
I see myself before myself
an arbiter of the bench
assessing the consequence
of outcome. The people of interest
who have lost said virtue
but somehow always
have the last word.
Who somehow always
accrue more sadness
than others and,
bidden or not,
steal into the stories
we tell ourselves
to drag ourselves
through these days
of errant demand.

the formerly so *(version)*

The odd verbs of mortality
pertain of late.
Clutter our texts,
our purposeful logs.
Disrupts our binge
w/dire ringtones
and finds us all,
the formerly so,
w/nothing to reveal
but the criminality
of our moments,
ripe w/ease.

borough jump

In the streets
the cri de coeur
is cranked to ten
As we borough jump
to Max's
to blast our ears
to smithereens.
And the cheap speed kicks in
as the city turns over
from dark to dawn
w/o a trace and
the humidity of rebellion
we once brought
to broken structures
has since been rebuilt
and priced way over
our fuckin heads

Her Own Forensic Design

She was perhaps, a taxi whore.
A rather rudimentary
simplex of things but
she was much more
than that: This daughter of a courtesan
and a priest not yet brought to heel,
had her own forensic design.
Her own depiction of the job it takes
to keep you clean. Her mayhem
and objective. Her glory and her glee.

Rejection 4 6 5

I've a hunch
this one's gonna
get away from me
as they often do
which you'd know
if you'd bothered
to read any or all
of the virgin editions
I stapled myself.

One of which
I recently rescued
from a book burning
(yeah, a book burning)
not too very
far from here.

The King of Questions

The king of questions
in dusky robes
(his army hungry,
  his generals moot)
sculpts the night
w/muscle and chrome,
as the whipping scarves
of Dulce Mia
pull his calculus
and she,
(modeled from the earth)
  eludes contours
the king's perspective
breathes ever so lightly
across his crown

flat blue tubes

On this side of mixed blessings
I answer the orphan starling.

Hold my mother's hand.

Seek the vulgar familiar.

Push air into flat blue tubes.

Mermaids sing high in the harbor.

A devoted lack of discipline
defines the poets day.

Manhattan Ash

The age
      of repair
            is upon me

Her secrets
      my scandal
            no syntax
              could tell

night flare

in the hour between
doing and done   my endeavors
earn no grace   my toe hold
on Heaven   shaky
at best

Seducing Vivaldi

Seducing Vivaldi
was easier than it seems
she said as if the red priest
hadn't been dead
for lo! so many years.

He may have been
one of the world's
great composers
she said speaking from
experience. But
he went down easy
like all men do.

Mitigation

This poem in need of mitigation
may hold your interest for a while
but, my dear cranky peers,
the truth is: Alerting you to urgency
has worn me out. Plugged in and captive
to the kabuki. The skirmish to balance
binder to pigment, poem to prayer.

Do we make history or endure it?
Who the fuck knows? Just give me
the provenance and let me decide
heads or tails before the coast erodes.
Before microbes rewrite our sacred texts.

irony

I needed to start a fire
so I bought my own book
back for a buck
and skinned
a small stray
for dinner.

Frog Eyes

Frog Eyes Fitzgerald
fought the foos
(those high flyin flashpoints
no one could catch)
in the war We won
he'd boast
after three bourbons
n a double rye
at the Fuselage
on 4th & Dyre.
The last great dive
that isn't
he'd say
Much like
so much
of this
fuckin country
he'd add
as Faye inveighed
Last call

Them quick as shit
lil motherfuckers
dooking, deeking,
so damn fast
you'd swear you never
took a breath!

Eyes bigger than mine

he'd assert

I know I know

Faye conveyed

I've seen

them little

fuckers too

n I wouldn't sleep

w/any of em

Like so much

of this fuckin country

she'd say

closing down

the night

My Meeting w/Vonnegut

There's an extremely bald guy
barking parking directions
from the fire tower
where I'm trying to call
upon a peaceful land
but I can't help thinking
I'm either gonna
push this guy
over the rail or
jump it and park
the car myself.
"You sow a sad intelligence,"
Kurt said, chronicling the inevitable.
"Here we are trapped in the amber
of the moment and you missed it"
his unfiltered lit, his eyes ignited.

Published globally, full length collections include the upcoming haiku collection, *Monet's Bamboo*, (CAPS Press, 2023), *mooncussers*, (Luchador Press 2022); *AmericanMental*, (Luchador Press 2020); *Blue Fan Whirring* (Nirala Press, 2018). Anthologies: *Calling All Poets 20th Anniversary Anthology*, (CAPS Press); *Reflecting Pool: Poets & the Creative Process* (Codhill Press, 2018); *Like Light: 25 Years of Poetry & Prose* (Bright Hill Press, 2018); others. Now in its 24th year, Mike serves as President of Calling All Poets, New Paltz, Beacon NY. A 2016 Pushcart nominee, online CD reviews appear at All About Jazz and Lightwoodpress.com Chairman, Music Fan Film Series, Rosendale Theater. Regional music and art features Van Wyck Gazette, 2013-2020. The Rock n Roll Curmudgeon appeared in Rhythm and News Magazine, 1996-2003.

This project was made possible, in part, by generous support from the Osage Arts Community.

Osage Arts Community provides temporary time, space and support for the creation of new artistic works in a retreat format, serving creative people of all kinds — visual artists, composers, poets, fiction and nonfiction writers. Located on a 152-acre farm in an isolated rural mountainside setting in Central Missouri and bordered by ¾ of a mile of the Gasconade River, OAC provides residencies to those working alone, as well as welcoming collaborative teams, offering living space and workspace in a country environment to emerging and mid-career artists. For more information, visit us at www.osageac.org

Osage Arts Community